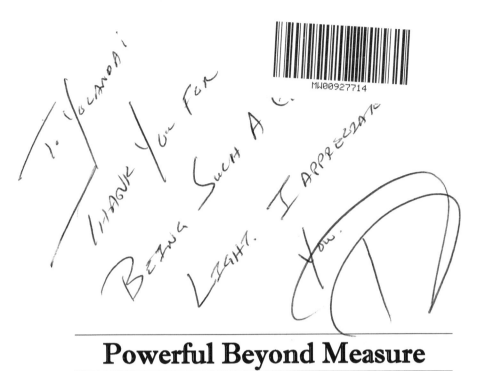

To Yolanda:
Thank You for
Being Such A ...
Light. I Appreciate
You.

Powerful Beyond Measure

Ryan L. Jones

Powerful Beyond Measure

This book was printed in the United States of America.

To order additional copies of this book, contact:

Ryan L. Jones & Associates, Inc
5220 Jimmy Lee Smith Parkway, Suite 104, #192
Hiram, Georgia 30141
678-549-6648
ryan@rljonesandassociates.net
www.rljonesandassociates.net

ISBN-13: 978-1523491698
ISBN-10:1523491698

DEDICATION

My family has shown me how To Be Powerful Beyond Measure as I am Achieving My Life's Purpose, Discovering My Best Self and knowing The Best That God Has For My Life....Thank You to my wife Karen and our children Rhyann Louise, Nigel Ryan, Omar Julian and Morgan Denise (you too Deon) and our grandson, Aiden Deon Wilson.

ACKNOWLEDGMENTS

The Leadership Team of the Empowerment Center...Iva Baldwin, Willa Jones, Antonio Ray, Kim Shivers and Phillip White for giving me an Optimistic Outlook; my brothers Tommy Ford, Tolton Pace, Bobby Reid, Hank Stewart and Jason Thomas for making me Release The Greatness Within; my mentees LaDarius Rashaad, Andrea Duncan and Dania Murrell for allowing me to be a "light" in your life; and those who took time to be my editors: Elisha Gray, Mindy Eisenhart-Howard and Wanjiku Kamuyu...THANK YOU.

AUTHOR'S NOTE

"...Our deepest fear is not that we are inadequate.
Our deepest fear is that we are powerful beyond measure."
(From *A Return To Love,* by Marianne Williamson)

What does it mean to be "Powerful Beyond Measure?" To me, it is about always and in all ways being open to becoming a life-long learner. Each day when I open my eyes, I ask the same question: "How can I be of service today?" Then I make the same statement: "Great things are going to happen to me, through me and for me today!"

I chose to put a picture of stones on the cover because I Peter 2:5 says, *"And you are living stones that God is building..."* All of us are living stones that are here to be used to build one another. I have seven sections in this book because (from a biblical meaning) it is a number of completeness, divine perfection or something that is finished. We complete one another and there power in the small stone. (Refer to 1 the Biblical story of David and Goliath in 1 Samuel 17)

Lastly, in each of the seven section, there are fifty quotes which represents the number I wore when I played basketball...#50.

It is my hope and prayer, that the power of these stones (words), will transmit, reflect, produce light and that you receive energy to remove the giant in your life...because you ARE Powerful Beyond Measure.

Ryan L. Jones

LIVE YOUR BEST LIFE NOW

DISCOVER YOUR BEST SELF

ACHIEVE YOUR LIFE'S PURPOSE

THE BEST THAT GOD HAS FOR
YOUR LIFE

INTENTIONALLY MANIFEST
WHAT YOU WANT

RELEASE THE GREATNESS
WITHIN

AN OPTIMISTIC OUTLOOK

LIVE YOUR BEST LIFE NOW

~#1~

To Be Powerful Beyond Measure and Live Your Best Life Now, is to not worry about how many/much Talents, Abilities, Gifts or Skills you are starting with; just begin with a million dollars' worth of Determination, Dedication and Desire.

~#2~

To Be Powerful Beyond Measure and Live Your Best Life Now, you must break the chains of mediocrity and find total fulfillment in and for your life.

~#3~

To Be Powerful Beyond Measure and Live Your Best Life Now, you need to Enlarge, Expand and Expect your vision. Go out and Conceive It, Believe It, Receive It and Achieve It!

~#4~

To Be Powerful Beyond Measure and Live Your Best Life Now, raise your level of Expectancy, Faith and Gratitude.

~#5~

To Be Powerful Beyond Measure and Live Your Best Life Now, is to intend to be happy!

~#6~

To Be Powerful Beyond Measure and Live Your Best Life Now, is to have a life of **MESS**....**M**anifested **E**xpectations (of) **S**piritual **S**atisfaction and **M**agnificent **E**xperiences (of) **S**atisfactory **S**uccess.

~#7~

To Be Powerful Beyond Measure and Live Your Best Life Now, is to be Addicted and Attracted to Confidence, Enthusiasm, Gratefulness, Happiness, Integrity, Love, Optimism, Peace, Success and

_____.

~#8~

To Be Powerful Beyond Measure and Live Your Best Life NOW, is to have an Attitude of Graditude knowing you are Fearfully and Wonderfully made.

~#9~

To Be Powerful Beyond Measure and Live Your Best Life Now, is to Concentrate, Meditate, Visualize and be Grateful for Intentional Meaningful Manifestation. Energy Flows Where Attention Goes.

~#10~

To Be Powerful Beyond Measure and Live Your Best Life Now, is to Consciously and Confidently be blessed and believe in God's Intentional Manifestation for/in your life.

~#11~

To Be Powerful Beyond Measure
and Live Your Best Life Now, you
MUST value yourself! VALUE
is...the [V]ision to take [A]ction
with [L]ove and [U]nderstanding so
you [E]volve.

~#12~

To Be Powerful Beyond Measure
and Live Your Best Life Now, means
living life your own way. It means
doing the things that gels with your
Heart, Mind and Soul. It means
learning to say no to the things you
no longer desire and say a
resounding YES to the things that
you do.

~#13~

To Be Powerful Beyond Measure
and Live Your Best Life Now, is to
Love yourself
UNCONDITIONALLY!

~#14~

To Be Powerful Beyond Measure
and Live Your Best Life Now, say
with authority "yeah" (or "yes")
which moves you towards your
highest being. When you follow
"yeah" with "but," you set yourself
up to be defeated.

~#15~

To Be Powerful Beyond Measure and Live Your Best Life Now, is to live your life freely, magnificently and awesome-ly. Do not live life half-way, do not live life ordinarily. Live life extraordinarily. Go big, bigger, best. Yes, when you live your best life you are living at the highest level of yourselves.

~#16~

To Be Powerful Beyond Measure and Live Your Best Life Now, is to be true to yourself.

~#17~

To Be Powerful Beyond Measure
and Live Your Best Life Now, is to
FOCUS (**F**ollow **O**ne **C**ourse **U**ntil
Successful) and **PUSH** (**P**ray **U**ntil
Something **H**appens) through the
FOG (**F**avor **O**f **G**od) until you
reach the **GAP** (**G**od **A**nswers
Prayers).

~#18~

To Be Powerful Beyond Measure
and Live Your Best Life Now, is to
feel the breeze of the "four winds of
success" blowing in your direction.
From North, South, East and West
will manifest your endless good.

~#19~

To Be Powerful Beyond Measure
and Live Your Best Life Now, is to
live Faithful, Fantabulous and
Flawsome.

~#20~

To Be Powerful Beyond Measure
and Live Your Best Life Now, is to
know you must be awake to your
good, and gather in the Harvest of
Endless Opportunities.

~#21~

To Be Powerful Beyond Measure and Live Your Best Life Now, is to have the ability to believe in yourself, which will make you a success in whatever you Desire, Do or Dream.

~#22~

To Be Powerful Beyond Measure and Live Your Best Life Now, is to let go of worn out conditions and circumstances. Divine order will be manifested in your conditions, circumstances, connections, commitments and character.

~#23~

To Be Powerful Beyond Measure
and Live Your Best Life Now, is to
not master the power of giving up,
giving in or giving out. What you do
is what you become!

~#24~

To Be Powerful Beyond Measure
and Live Your Best Life Now, is to
know "you are the Power, Purpose,
Potential and Promises you believe
you are.

~#25~

To Be Powerful Beyond Measure and Live Your Best Life Now, is to know you are born in the image and likeness of God's Greatness. The world gains little from your self-imposed smallness but it gains much more when you allow your Greatness to shine. Think Big, Do Great things and Celebrate your Uniqueness.

~#26~

To Be Powerful Beyond Measure and Live Your Best Life Now, is to EXPECT the good and the great things to happen! Have an Optimistic outlook because energy flows where attention goes.

~#27~

To Be Powerful Beyond Measure
and Live Your Best Life Now, is to
speak good things over your life and
believe that they will manifest.
Release your faith and your words,
believing in God's Favor.

~#28~

To Be Powerful Beyond Measure
and Live Your Best Life Now, you
MUST Enlarge, Expand and Expect
your Values (what you show),
Vision (what you see) and Voice
(what you say) to be manifested.

~#29~

To Be Powerful Beyond Measure
and Live Your Best Life Now, is to
know that there is nothing cheap
about you at all! God's creative,
artistic, intelligent genius went into
creating the Best and Blessed of
who YOU are.

~#30~

To Be Powerful Beyond Measure
and Live Your Best Life Now, you
have to know that God will take
your ordinary and do extraordinary
things.

~#31~

To Be Powerful Beyond Measure
and Live Your Best Life Now, you
must know in order to get more,
you have to give more.

~#32~

To Be Powerful Beyond Measure
and Live Your Best Life Now, you
must NEVER give in, give up or give
out but ALWAYS in ALL WAYS give
all you have to give.

~#33~

To Be Powerful Beyond Measure
and Live Your Best Life Now, is to
surround yourself with people who
will Complete you, not deplete you.

~#34~

To Be Powerful Beyond Measure
and Live Your Best Life Now, is to
know your best days are not behind
you...but your Blessed days are in
front of you.

~#35~

To Be Powerful Beyond Measure
and Live Your Best Life Now, is to
live your life by design and not by
default. Stepping out of your
comfort zone is uncomfortable, but
it can make what seems impossible,
possible.

~#36~

To Be Powerful Beyond Measure and Live Your Best Life Now, you need to possess an Attitude of Gratitude. God has brand-new blessings for you and you ought to find yourself being grateful for the Plans, Positions, Possibilities, Promises, Promotions, Provisions and Purposes to be manifested in your life.

~#37~

To Be Powerful Beyond Measure and Live Your Best Life Now, is to have the will to **WIN**...**W**ant **I**t **N**ow! Your Will verses your wants makes you execute the plan relentlessly.

~#38~

To Be Powerful Beyond Measure and Live Your Best Life Now, is to know the power of *WE* is much stronger than the power of me.

~#39~

To Be Powerful Beyond Measure
and Live Your Best Life Now, is to
have the Belief to "Believe It In"
that which you "believe in" or
"believe on."

~#40~

To Be Powerful Beyond Measure
and Live Your Best Life Now, is
Saying it, Believing it and Knowing
it shall be Manifested in your life.
You become effective by becoming
selective.

~#41~

To Be Powerful Beyond Measure
and Live Your Best Life Now, you
have the power to bring about all
the Intentional and Positive
changes in your life you desire.

~#42~

To Be Powerful Beyond Measure
and Live Your Best Life Now, you
have the right to see reflected in
that Manifesting mirror whatever
you want to be, do or have.

~#43~

To Be Powerful Beyond Measure and Live Your Best Life Now, is to know that no matter how untalented you feel compared to others, God created you to be something spectacular. It is already part of your very essence.

~#44~

To Be Powerful Beyond Measure and Live Your Best Life Now, is to make the transition from "anticipation and hoping" for the manifestation to "living in" and "seeing" the manifestation.

~#45~

To Be Powerful Beyond Measure
and Live Your Best Life Now, is to
have Intentional Now Faith,
Through Faith and By Faith for
your Expectancies to be Manifested.

~#46~

To Be Powerful Beyond Measure
and Live Your Best Life Now, is to
Live your life passionately and
powerfully Always and in All Ways
in 100% Forward
MOTION...**M**oving, **O**ptimistic,
Tenacious, **I**ntentional,
Operational, **N**ow.

~#47~

To Be Powerful Beyond Measure
and Live Your Best Life Now, is to
Elevation requires Action,
Dedication, Direction, Imagination,
Inspiration, Meditation,
Motivation, Realization,
Perspiration, Preparation,
Transformation and Visualization.

~#48~

To Be Powerful Beyond Measure
and Live Your Best Life Now, is to
Live your Life by Design and not by
default. It needs to be out **LOUD**
(**L**oved, **O**ptimistic, **U**nique,
Determined). You are Living On
Purpose, With A Purpose and For A
Purpose.

~#49~

To Be Powerful Beyond Measure and Live Your Best Life Now, is to know you are more Significant and Magnificent than anything that you can imagine. You will journey to that place of self-evolution when you give yourself permission to move beyond being ordinary to Extraordinary.

~#50~

To Be Powerful Beyond Measure and Live Your Best Life Now, is Living your life Boldly, Bravely and Beautifully should be your utmost priority. When you live your life for yourself, you will have so much more to share with others. Live your life Passionately and Compassionately without holding back.

DISCOVER YOUR BEST SELF

~#1~

To Be Powerful Beyond Measure
and Discover Your Best Self, is to
allow the space between where you
are and where you want to be,
Inspire you not intimidate you.

~#2~

To Be Powerful Beyond Measure
and Discover Your Best Self, is to be
a Prayer Warrior not a prayer
worrier. You cannot pray about it
and worry about it.

~#3~

To Be Powerful Beyond Measure and Discover Your Best Self, is to know the best place to be for your Promises to prevail is in the middle of God's Plan and Purpose for your life.

~#4~

To Be Powerful Beyond Measure and Discover Your Best Self, is to pray on it, pray over it, pray about it, pray for it...but most of all, PRAY THROUGH IT!

~#5~

To Be Powerful Beyond Measure and Discover Your Best Self, is to not allow what has happened in the past, cause you to miss out on what God is doing in your life right now. This is your NOW season.

~#6~

To Be Powerful Beyond Measure and Discover Your Best Self, is being able to manifest absolutely anything and create the life YOU truly want and desire and - dare I say it - deserve.

~#7~

To Be Powerful Beyond Measure and Discover Your Best Self, is to know when God calls you to YOUR Purpose and Plan, He will provide you with all the necessary requirements to accomplish and achieve it.

~#8~

To Be Powerful Beyond Measure and Discover Your Best Self, is to know what God has for you, is for YOU.

~#9~

To Be Powerful Beyond Measure
and Discover Your Best Self, is to
know you have something to live
for, not only with.

~#10~

To Be Powerful Beyond Measure
and Discover Your Best Self, is
seeing your greatness and goodness
while shifting your perspective to
allow new possibilities.

~#11~

To Be Powerful Beyond Measure
and Discover Your Best Self, is to
know you are Moving Forward
when you become uninterested in
looking (or going) back.

~#12~

To Be Powerful Beyond Measure
and Discover Your Best Self, is to
know you will Do BIG things for
yourself when you See BIG things
for yourself.

~#13~

To Be Powerful Beyond Measure and Discover Your Best Self, is to know if you are not willing to change do not expect your life to change.

~#14~

To Be Powerful Beyond Measure and Discover Your Best Self, is to know to get a new beginning you need a new ending! Speak about what you DO want MORE of and what you DO want LESS of?

~#15~

To Be Powerful Beyond Measure and Discover Your Best Self, is to spend your time is one of the most valuable assets you have. Do not let others waste it by spending serious time with casual people.

~#16~

To Be Powerful Beyond Measure and Discover Your Best Self, is to know Fear Reacts...Faith Acts.

~#17~

To Be Powerful Beyond Measure
and Discover Your Best Self, is to
know what God has for you in your
future is greater than what you have
experienced in the past. Take the
limits off!

~#18~

To Be Powerful Beyond Measure
and Discover Your Best Self, is to do
something! We have a tendency to
think situations will correct
themselves, but nothing changes if
nothing changes!

~#19~

To Be Powerful Beyond Measure
and Discover Your Best Self, is to
not get so busy loving everyone else
that you forget to love yourself.

~20~

To Be Powerful Beyond Measure
and Discover Your Best Self, is to
know one of the most powerful
phrases in the world is "I am."

~#21~

To Be Powerful Beyond Measure and Discover Your Best Self, is to know before you talk, listen. Before you react, think. Before you criticize, wait. Before you pray, forgive. Before you quit, try.

~#22~

To Be Powerful Beyond Measure and Discover Your Best Self, is to live your life knowing that you are not perfect, than spending your whole life pretending to be.

~#23~

To Be Powerful Beyond Measure and Discover Your Best Self, is to know the things you think about, focus on, and surround yourselves with will shape who you become.

~#24~

To Be Powerful Beyond Measure and Discover Your Best Self, is to know God turns broken pieces into MASTERPIECES!

~#25~

To Be Powerful Beyond Measure
and Discover Your Best Self, is to
know you do not have to be great in
God. You just have to let God be
great in you.

~#26~

To Be Powerful Beyond Measure
and Discover Your Best Self, is to
know it is always better to get a
"peace" of mind than to always give
a "piece" of mind.

~#27~

To Be Powerful Beyond Measure
and Discover Your Best Self, is to
know people with the worst past
create the best future!

~#28~

To Be Powerful Beyond Measure
and Discover Your Best Self, is to
speak what you expect.

~#29~

To Be Powerful Beyond Measure
and Discover Your Best Self, is to be
a person who can lay a firm
foundation with the bricks others
have thrown at him.

~#30~

To Be Powerful Beyond Measure
and Discover Your Best Self, is to
not feel sad over someone who gave
up on you, feel sorry for them
because they gave up on someone
who would have never given up on
them.

~#31~

To Be Powerful Beyond Measure
and Discover Your Best Self, is to
know when you are tired, draw
strength from God. When you are
speechless, talk to God. When you
are lonely, there is God.

~#32~

To Be Powerful Beyond Measure
and Discover Your Best Self, is to
know you may have gone through
something that has changed you in
a way that you could never go back
to the person you once were.

~#33~

To Be Powerful Beyond Measure
and Discover Your Best Self, is to
not raise your voice to improve your
argument.

~#34~

To Be Powerful Beyond Measure
and Discover Your Best Self, is to
stop running away from your
problems, because that only
increases the distance from the
solution.

~#35~

To Be Powerful Beyond Measure and Discover Your Best Self, is to know you have to stop worrying. Have faith that things will work out. Maybe not how you planned, but just how they are supposed to be.

~#36~

To Be Powerful Beyond Measure and Discover Your Best Self, is to know the closer you get to your destination the greater your distraction.

~#37~

To Be Powerful Beyond Measure
and Discover Your Best Self, is to
know sometimes you have to get
knocked down lower than you have
ever been, to stand up taller than
you than you ever were.

~#38~

To Be Powerful Beyond Measure
and Discover Your Best Self, is to
know the greatest mistake you can
make in life is to continually fear
you will make one.

~#39~

To Be Powerful Beyond Measure
and Discover Your Best Self, is to
know you will never have what you
are not willing to pursue.

~#40~

To Be Powerful Beyond Measure
and Discover Your Best Self, is to
forget what hurt you, but never
forget what it taught you.

~#41~

To Be Powerful Beyond Measure
and Discover Your Best Self, is to
always and in all ways bring your
"A" game...Ability, Ambition,
Appreciation, Attention, Attitude,
Authentic and Awareness.

~#42~

To Be Powerful Beyond Measure
and Discover Your Best Self, is to be
a Thermostat who regulates the
temperature of the environment
instead of a Thermometer who
reflects the temperature of the
environment.

~#43~

To Be Powerful Beyond Measure
and Discover Your Best Self, is to
know it is better to have a life of
'OH WELLS' than a life of 'WHAT
IFS.'

~#44~

To Be Powerful Beyond Measure
and Discover Your Best Self, is to
know that Faith sees the thing that
is missing, instead of seeing that
something is missing.

~#45~

To Be Powerful Beyond Measure
and Discover Your Best Self, is to
know that you can become someone
the whole world might know if your
Dream is big enough and you walk
in your Destiny.

~#46~

To Be Powerful Beyond Measure
and Discover Your Best Self, is to
have Determination, Dedication,
Focus, Gratitude, Optimism and
Perseverance to Empower your life
to your level of Excellence.

~#47~

To Be Powerful Beyond Measure and Discover Your Best Self, is to KNOW you are Unique and Possess the Power to Create, Take Action, Make Choices and Have as well as Be what you Desire.

~#48~

To Be Powerful Beyond Measure and Discover Your Best Self, is to be Grateful and Gracious not only for your NOW (experience) but your NEXT (expectation).

~#49~

To Be Powerful Beyond Measure and Discover Your Best Self, is to stop making time for the things you do not want to do and excuses for the things you need to do.

~#50~

To Be Powerful Beyond Measure and Discover Your Best Self, is to know you are what your deepest desire is. As your desire is, so is your INTENTION. As your Intention is, so is your INFLUENCE. As your Influence is, so is your ILLUMINATION. As your Illumination is, so is your IMPACT.

ACHIEVE YOUR LIFE'S PURPOSE

~#1~

To Be Powerful Beyond Measure
and Achieve Your Life's Purpose, is
to achieve success by believing in
yourself by being Consistent
(unchanging), Insistent
(unrelenting), Persistent
(unyielding) and Resistant
(unaffected).

~#2~

To Be Powerful Beyond Measure
and Achieve Your Life's Purpose, is
to know without great risk, there is
no great reward.

~#3~

To Be Powerful Beyond Measure and Achieve Your Life's Purpose, is to use your intuition to hear the messages behind the words. If you feel something inside, you are probably listening with your heart.

~#4~

To Be Powerful Beyond Measure and Achieve Your Life's Purpose, is to know your intentional prayer is not just what you desire, but also what you continually, fervently and without relenting focus on to be manifested.

~#5~

To Be Powerful Beyond Measure
and Achieve Your Life's Purpose, is
to know God has a Purpose and
Plan for your Fearfully and
Wonderfully created life. Your eyes
will see, your ears will hear and
your heart will feel the things God
has prepared for and promised you.

~#6~

To Be Powerful Beyond Measure
and Achieve Your Life's Purpose, is
to know you are an ordinary person
with extraordinary power; you are a
natural person who can live a
supernatural life.

~#7~

To Be Powerful Beyond Measure
and Achieve Your Life's Purpose, is
to know God will send people to
Sharpen, Show, Strengthen,
Stretch, Support and Supply
you...but NOT to steal from you or
stall you.

~#8~

To Be Powerful Beyond Measure
and Achieve Your Life's Purpose, is
to have Consistent Spiritual
Growth, Persistent Personal
Development and Sufficient Self-
Improvement.

~#9~

To Be Powerful Beyond Measure and Achieve Your Life's Purpose, is to KNOW you are sentenced to succeed. So walk out of your mess and into God's Will for your BLESSED and BEST Success.

~#10~

To Be Powerful Beyond Measure and Achieve Your Life's Purpose, is to not wait to SEE what happens in your life, but SAY what happens in it. SPEAK LIFE!!!

~#11~

To Be Powerful Beyond Measure and Achieve Your Life's Purpose, is to know Growth and Change are painful. But nothing is as painful as staying somewhere you do not belong.

~#12~

To Be Powerful Beyond Measure and Achieve Your Life's Purpose, is to know you may not have your dream life at this moment, but each day it is worth striving to reach toward that dream to make it a reality.

~#13~

To Be Powerful Beyond Measure and Achieve Your Life's Purpose, is to be careful who you call your friends. You should rather have 4 quarters than 100 pennies.

~#14~

To Be Powerful Beyond Measure and Achieve Your Life's Purpose, is to not forgive people because you are weak. You forgive them because you are strong enough to know people make mistakes.

~#15~

To Be Powerful Beyond Measure
and Achieve Your Life's Purpose, is
to know one of the good things
about goodbye, is that it means you
are a little closer to a new hello.

~#16~

To Be Powerful Beyond Measure
and Achieve Your Life's Purpose, is
to know life is not about people who
act true to your face. It is about
people who remain true behind
your back.

~#17~

To Be Powerful Beyond Measure
and Achieve Your Life's Purpose, is
to know you will never become who
you want to be if you keep blaming
everyone else for who you are.

~#18~

To Be Powerful Beyond Measure
and Achieve Your Life's Purpose, is
to not leave room in your future for
people who left you in their past.

~#19~

To Be Powerful Beyond Measure
and Achieve Your Life's Purpose, is
to use your smile to change this
world. Do not let this world change
your smile.

~#20~

To Be Powerful Beyond Measure
and Achieve Your Life's Purpose, is
to know you have three choices in
life, GIVE IN, GIVE UP, OR GIVE
IT YOUR ALL.

~#21~

To Be Powerful Beyond Measure
and Achieve Your Life's Purpose, is
to know you do not stop dreaming
and exploring because you grew
old. You grow old because you
stopped dreaming and exploring.

~#22~

To Be Powerful Beyond Measure
and Achieve Your Life's Purpose, is
to be so busy loving you and your
life that you have no time for hate
or regret.

~#23~

To Be Powerful Beyond Measure and Achieve Your Life's Purpose, is to not use your past as an excuse to miss out on your future.

~#24~

To Be Powerful Beyond Measure and Achieve Your Life's Purpose, is to know who you are around helps determine where you are going to go.

~#25~

To Be Powerful Beyond Measure
and Achieve Your Life's Purpose, is
to not force what (or who) does not
FIT in your life!

~#26~

To Be Powerful Beyond Measure
and Achieve Your Life's Purpose, is
to stop focusing on what "wasn't"
and start focusing on what will be!

~#27~

To Be Powerful Beyond Measure and Achieve Your Life's Purpose, is to know God has more ahead of you than what was behind you! Stay moving forward and Focused in Faith and watch what is getting ready to happen!

~#28~

To Be Powerful Beyond Measure and Achieve Your Life's Purpose, is to know the FAVOR upon your life may FRUSTRATE others of their attitude of envy. But do not let that deter you from walking in the blessings of GOD.

~#29~

To Be Powerful Beyond Measure
and Achieve Your Life's Purpose, is
to know God does not break things
so God can fix them; God fixes
broken things so God can use them.

~#30~

To Be Powerful Beyond Measure
and Achieve Your Life's Purpose, is
to know worrying not only distracts
you, it attracts the things you do not
want.

~#31~

To Be Powerful Beyond Measure
and Achieve Your Life's Purpose, is
to know before you can be a "plus
one" you have to learn how to be
"just one" and you have to learn to
master 'ME' before you can master
'WE'.

~#32~

To Be Powerful Beyond Measure
and Achieve Your Life's Purpose, is
to STOP looking for happiness in
the same place that you LOST it.

~#33~

To Be Powerful Beyond Measure
and Achieve Your Life's Purpose, is
to know success does not happen by
accident. It happens by your
Actions.

~#34~

To Be Powerful Beyond Measure
and Achieve Your Life's Purpose, is
to speak what you seek until you see
what you have said!

~#35~

To Be Powerful Beyond Measure
and Achieve Your Life's Purpose, is
to make good on your "good
intentions". Things will continue to
remain "in tension" until you do
what you INTEND to do.

~#36~

To Be Powerful Beyond Measure
and Achieve Your Life's Purpose, is
to let the past be the past and not let
it destroy your future. Live life for
what tomorrow has to offer, not for
what yesterday has taken away.

~#37~

To Be Powerful Beyond Measure
and Achieve Your Life's Purpose, is
to know scars remind us of where
we have been but do not have to
dictate where we are going.

~#38~

To Be Powerful Beyond Measure
and Achieve Your Life's Purpose, is
to know even if you cannot get it
perfect, you can still get it done.

~#39~

To Be Powerful Beyond Measure
and Achieve Your Life's Purpose, is
to Overwhelm the overwhelming
circumstances without being
overwhelmed.

~#40~

To Be Powerful Beyond Measure
and Achieve Your Life's Purpose, is
to not exchange what you want the
MOST for what you want at the
moment.

~#41~

To Be Powerful Beyond Measure and Achieve Your Life's Purpose, is to know when you focus on problems, you will have more problems. When you focus on possibilities, you will have more opportunities.

~#42~

To Be Powerful Beyond Measure and Achieve Your Life's Purpose, is to know you have never really lived until you have done something for someone who can never repay you.

~#43~

To Be Powerful Beyond Measure
and Achieve Your Life's Purpose, is
to Thank God for giving you
another chance at life by providing
a new day to get it right.

~#44~

To Be Powerful Beyond Measure
and Achieve Your Life's Purpose, is
to know falling down is a part of
life, getting back up is living.

~#45~

To Be Powerful Beyond Measure
and Achieve Your Life's Purpose, is
to stop thinking about what you are
missing, but thinking about what
you have that everyone else is
missing.

~#46~

To Be Powerful Beyond Measure
and Live Your Life's Purpose, is to
remember there is an Opportunity
in every obstacle.

~#47~

To Be Powerful Beyond Measure and Achieve Your Life's Purpose, is to know the four life changing words you can say to another person are I BELIEVE IN YOU... Make sure you say them to yourself as well.

~#48~

To Be Powerful Beyond Measure and Live Your Life's Purpose, is to know the past is a place of Reference, not a place of Residence.

~#49~

To Be Powerful Beyond Measure
and Achieve Your Life's Purpose, is
to not get comfortable in the place
you need to be careful. Remember,
everyone in your circle is not in
your corner.

~#50~

To Be Powerful Beyond Measure
and Achieve Your Life's Purpose, is
to Reach Upward, Open Inward so
you can Expand Outward to awaken
your Authentic, Original,
Custom/Tailor-Made, One-Of-A-
Kind Self. Expect to Expand and
Expand to Expect.

THE BEST THAT GOD HAS FOR YOUR LIFE

~#1~

To Manifest The Best That God Has For Your Life, is to know He has the unique ability to ensure that you get what you need – while you share what you have.

~#2~

To Manifest The Best That God Has For Your Life, is to think, speak and take action of and for what you want to do, be and have.

~#3~

To Manifest The Best That God Has For Your Life, is unleashing and letting go of the restraints that have limited you from your Dreams, Desires and Destiny.

~#4~

To Manifest The Best That God Has For Your Life, is to deliberately, exceptionally and proactively make the choice to live your life by design and not by default.

~#5~

To Manifest The Best That God Has For Your Life, is to have what you speak instead of speaking of what you have.

~#6~

To Manifest The Best That God Has For Your Life, is to be Grateful, Appreciative and Thankful (and KNOW) that His Plan, Power, Promises, Promotion, Protection, Provision and Purpose WILL be Unleashed in an Upward, Unprecedented, Unlimited, Unique way.

~#7~

To Manifest The Best That God Has For Your Life, is to know Gratitude and Acknowledgement are essential components in creating and attracting what you want into your life.

~#8~

To Manifest The Best That God Has For Your Life, is to not stay HERE when THERE is calling you. PREPARE for what is BEFORE you instead of trying to REPAIR what is BEHIND you.

~#9~

To Manifest The Best That God Has For Your Life, is to know you cannot always wait for something to happen, you have to be the one to make it happen.

~#10~

To Manifest The Best That God Has For Your Life, is to think big, dream big, believe big...and the results will be big!

~#11~

To Manifest The Best That God Has For Your Life, is to know you make a living by what you get; you make a life by what you give.

~#12~

To Manifest The Best That God Has For Your Life, is to be thankful for what you have; you will end up having more. If you concentrate on what you do not have, you will never, ever have enough.

~#13~

To Manifest The Best That God Has
For Your Life, is to know good
things come to those who believe,
Better things come to those who
wait and the Best things come to
those who do not give up.

~#14~

To Manifest The Best That God Has
For Your Life, is to know things
turn out best for the people who
make the best of the way things
turn out.

~#15~

To Manifest The Best That God Has For Your Life, is to know not only does prayer change things, but to know that prayer changes you and you change things.

~#16~

To Manifest The Best That God Has For Your Life, is to know no matter what happens, no matter how far you seem to be away from where you want to be, never stop believing that you will make it.

~#17~

To Manifest The Best That God Has For Your Life, is to not spend your nights dreaming about the life you want to live, but live your dreams and spend the night sleeping.

~#18~

To Manifest The Best That God Has For Your Life, is to know if it does not challenge you, it does not change you.

~#19~

To Manifest The Best That God Has For Your Life, is to use the rocks people throw at you to build the bridge to cross into your Destiny.

~#20~

To Manifest The Best That God Has For Your Life, is to let go of the things that needlessly complicate your life.

~#21~

To Manifest The Best That God Has For Your Life, is to know you have the power to Accomplish and Live great things. Do not stand Begging for that which you have the power to Achieve and Receive.

~#22~

To Manifest The Best That God Has For Your Life, is to know you know you are Moving Forward when you become uninterested in looking back.

~#23~

To Manifest The Best That God Has For Your Life, is to not let life change your goals, because achieving your goals can change your life.

~#24~

To Manifest The Best That God Has For Your Life, is to know Access is better than acquisition. You do not have to own it if you can get to it.

~#25~

To Manifest The Best That God Has For Your Life, is to stop saying "I wish" and start saying "I will".

~#26~

To Manifest The Best That God Has For Your Life, is to know you cannot fall if you do not climb, but there is no joy in living your whole life on the ground.

~#27~

To Manifest The Best That God Has For Your Life, is to know your value does not decrease based on someone's inability to see your worth!

~#28~

To Manifest The Best That God Has For Your Life, is to Be Beautiful, Better, Blessed, Brilliant and Bold. This is the time for YOU to breakout and breakthrough those things that tried to hold you in bondage.

~#29~

To Manifest The Best That God Has For Your Life, is to know life is about becoming a better version of yourself.

~#30~

To Manifest The Best That God Has For Your Life, is to know your value does not decrease based on someone's inability to see your worth!

~#31~

To Manifest The Best That God Has For Your Life, is to know a "trying time" is not a reason to quit trying.

~#32~

To Manifest The Best That God Has For Your Life, is to count your Blessings, not your burdens.

~#33~

To Manifest The Best That God Has For Your Life, is to concentrate on your strengths instead of your struggles, on your powers instead of your problems.

~#34~

To Manifest The Best That God Has For Your Life, is to know life is about becoming a better, best and bold version of yourself.

~#35~

To Manifest The Best That God Has For Your Life, is to give without remembering and always in all ways receive without forgetting.

~#36~

To Manifest The Best That God Has For Your Life, is to have a Vision that is Obtainable and Sustainable.

~#37~

To Manifest The Best That God Has For Your Life, is to Enlarge, Expand and Expect your vision. Go out and Conceive It, Believe It, Receive It and Achieve It!

~#38~

To Manifest The Best That God Has For Your Life, is to KNOW the power of your thoughts and words. Your thoughts determine your Actions, Attitude and Altitude.

~#39~

To Manifest The Best That God Has For Your Life, is to Love the person you have become...because you have become the person that you Love.

~#40~

To Manifest The Best That God Has For Your Life, is to focus on your Promise and not your problems. Energy flows where focused attention goes.

~#41~

To Manifest The Best That God Has For Your Life, is to KNOW you were born an Original, Custom, Fearfully and Wonderfully Tailor-Made, One-Of-A-Kind Creation....do not die a copy or duplicate of someone else

~#42~

To Manifest The Best That God Has For Your Life, is to ALWAYS and in ALL WAYS know that good comes to you in a steady, unbroken, ever-increasing stream of success, happiness and abundance.

~#43~

To Manifest The Best That God Has
For Your Life, is to RE-
up...REcharge your Passion,
REduce your Pain, REfocus on your
Perspective, REinforce your
Purpose, RElease your Past,
REmember your Promise, REmove
your Problems, REspect your
Potential, REstore your Power,
REveal your Possibilities and
REjoice in your Praise.

~#44~

To Manifest The Best That God Has For Your Life, is to know that this is your season of EXPECTANCY to Expand, Enlarge, Explode and Execute exceedingly abundantly above all that you ask or think according to the power (faith) that works in you.

~#45~

To Manifest The Best That God Has For Your Life, is to know that He has the power to cancel your past, conquer your problems, change your personality and complete your purpose.

~#46~

To Manifest The Best That God Has For Your Life, is to know that the Spirit has called us to ministry to: Affect (change), Effect (cause) and Infect (contagious). Let your light shine to make a difference in someone else's life.

~#47~

To Manifest The Best That God Has For Your Life, is to get up every morning with Determination; talk to Inspiration; bathe in Affirmation; spend the day with Expectation; have a nightcap with Celebration and go to bed with Satisfaction.

~#48~

To Manifest The Best That God Has For Your Life, is to go on an Appreciation Rampage. Be intentional as you grow, show and sow your Expressions, Gratitude, Kindness, Pleasantries and Thankfulness for your life getting better and better and better.

~#49~

To Manifest The Best That God Has For Your Life, is to let the ground you are on be Abundant, Blessed, Confident, Determined, Expectant and Favored Ground. The Ground you are on is _____ ground.

~#50~

To Manifest The Best That God Has For Your Life, is to know Your Want, Will, Work and Worth should be Consistent (unchanging), Insistent (unrelenting), Persistent (unyielding) and Resistant (unaffected).

INTENTIONALLY MANIFEST
WHAT YOU WANT

~#1~

To Be Powerful Beyond Measure
and Intentionally Manifest What
You Want, is to Always keep your
head up, because if it is down you
will not be able to see the blessings
that have been placed in your life.

~#2~

To Be Powerful Beyond Measure
and Intentionally Manifest What
You Want, is to know wishing will
NEVER be a substitute for prayer.

~#3~

To Be Powerful Beyond Measure and Intentionally Manifest What You Want, is to do something now that will make the person you'll be tomorrow proud to have been the person you are today.

~#4~

To Be Powerful Beyond Measure and Intentionally Manifest What You Want, is to prove yourself to yourself not others.

~#5~

To Be Powerful Beyond Measure
and Intentionally Manifest What
You Want, is to let your past make
you BETTER not BITTER.

~#6~

To Be Powerful Beyond Measure
and Intentionally Manifest What
You Want, is to know a PESSIMIST
sees the difficulty in every
opportunity, and OPTIMIST sees
the opportunity in every difficulty.

~#7~

To Be Powerful Beyond Measure
and Intentionally Manifest What
You Want, is to know a great life is
not about BIG things, it is about the
small things that make a big
difference.

~#8~

To Be Powerful Beyond Measure
and Intentionally Manifest What
You Want, is to know you can lose
yourselves in the things you love.
More importantly, find yourselves
there, too.

~#9~

To Be Powerful Beyond Measure and Intentionally Manifest What You Want, is to value who you have in life rather than what you have in life.

~#10~

To Be Powerful Beyond Measure and Intentionally Manifest What You Want, is to Be a Warrior in Faith not a worrier in fear.

~#11~

To Be Powerful Beyond Measure
and Intentionally Manifest What
You Want, is to know every test in
your life makes you bitter or better.
Every problem comes to break you
or make you. The choice is yours be
the victim or the Victor.

~#12~

To Be Powerful Beyond Measure
and Intentionally Manifest What
You Want, is to know God's Will
(His Plan) is in God Will (His
Promise).

~#13~

To Be Powerful Beyond Measure and Intentionally Manifest What You Want, is to know every day will be a great day, which becomes a great month, which becomes a great year, which becomes YOUR GREAT, GREATER and GREATEST Life.

~#14~

To Be Powerful Beyond Measure and Intentionally Manifest What You Want, is to know because God is the "I Am That I Am," ...I am.

~#15~

To Be Powerful Beyond Measure and Intentionally Manifest What You Want, is to be a Significant Strong Voice, not an insignificant weak echo.

~#16~

To Be Powerful Beyond Measure and Intentionally Manifest What You Want, is to know the Upside is you do not have to stand on the Outside staring at the Downside of what God is doing on the Inside.

~#17~

To Be Powerful Beyond Measure
and Intentionally Manifest What
You Want, is to Focus on what is
holding you together instead of
what is tearing you apart.

~#18~

To Be Powerful Beyond Measure
and Intentionally Manifest What
You Want, is to know every test in
your life makes you Better not
bitter; every problem comes to
Make you not break you. You ARE
the Victor not the victim.

~#19~

To Be Powerful Beyond Measure and Intentionally Manifest What You Want, is to have the will to WIN...Want It Now! Your Will should be Consistent (unchanging), Insistent (unrelenting), Persistent (unyielding) and Resistant (unaffected)...be relentlessly.

~#20~

To Be Powerful Beyond Measure and Intentionally Manifest What You Want, is to know if you want something bad enough, you have to be a BEAST (Believe It, Expect It, Anticipate It, Speak It, Think It) to get it!

~#21~

To Be Powerful Beyond Measure and Intentionally Manifest What You Want, is to know what you make happen for others, God will make happen for you.

~#22~

To Be Powerful Beyond Measure and Intentionally Manifest What You Want, is to be Grateful for people who Deposit, Impart, Pour and Sow seeds of Abundance, Blessings and Greatness into your life.

~#23~

To Be Powerful Beyond Measure
and Intentionally Manifest What
You Want, is to know when you
stop chasing the wrong things you
give the right things a chance to
catch you.

~#24~

To Be Powerful Beyond Measure
and Intentionally Manifest What
You Want, is to replace your 'trying'
with the full commitment of
DOING.

~#25~

To Be Powerful Beyond Measure
and Intentionally Manifest What
You Want, is to know in order to be
Great is to be Grateful and
Gracious.

~#26~

To Be Powerful Beyond Measure
and Intentionally Manifest What
You Want, is to know that you must
Expect great things of yourself
before you can Experience them.

~#27~

To Be Powerful Beyond Measure
and Intentionally Manifest What
You Want, is to know that your
Head can Conceive it; your Heart
can Believe it; your Hope can
Achieve it and your Hands will
Receive it.

~#28~

To Be Powerful Beyond Measure
and Intentionally Manifest What
You Want, is to live with Courage,
Commitment and Confidence to
operate at the higher level.

~#29~

To Be Powerful Beyond Measure
and Intentionally Manifest What
You Want, is to know you are better
than you were and you are better
than you are.

~#30~

To Be Powerful Beyond Measure
and Intentionally Manifest What
You Want, is to be a **GOAL**
{**G**reater **O**pportunities (&)
Abundant **L**iving} Digger.

~#31~

To Be Powerful Beyond Measure
and Intentionally Manifest What
You Want, is to find yourself in your
Purpose and Passion in the things
you love, not to lose yourself there.

~#32~

To Be Powerful Beyond Measure
and Intentionally Manifest What
You Want, means creating your life
by design not by default. You were
born on purpose, with a purpose
and for a purpose. You become
Effective by being Selective.
Remember, energy flows where
attention goes.

~#33~

To Be Powerful Beyond Measure
and Intentionally Manifest What
You Want, is to do something that
people will Appreciate, Celebrate,
Duplicate, Elevate, Illuminate,
Imitate, Replicate and Simulate.

~#34~

To Be Powerful Beyond Measure
and Intentionally Manifest What
You Want, is to know that
everything you have ever wanted is
on the other side of fear.

~#35~

To Be Powerful Beyond Measure and Intentionally Manifest What You Want, is to be Thankful to and Trust in God.

~#36~

To Be Powerful Beyond Measure is to know God was not having a bad day when you were created. You are Fearfully and Wonderfully made to Intentionally Manifest What You Want and What You Are Worth.

~#37~

To Be Powerful Beyond Measure
and Intentionally Manifest What
You Want, is to live a Faithful,
Fearless and Forward Focused Life
by demonstrating the true power of
LOVE in your Actions, Articulation,
Atmosphere and Attitude.

~#38~

To Be Powerful Beyond Measure
and Intentionally Manifest What
You Want, is to step forward or you
will always remain in the same
place.

~#39~

To Be Powerful Beyond Measure is to know in order to Intentionally Manifest What You Want, is to have the Confidence and Courage to get rid of and let go of what you do not want/need.

~#40~

To Be Powerful Beyond Measure and Intentionally Manifest What You Want, is to wake up everyday with limitless opportunities in front of you and the ability to turn them into solid results.

~#41~

To Be Powerful Beyond Measure
and Intentionally Manifest What
You Want, is to Speak what you
Seek until you See and Seize what
you have Said and Say.

~#42~

To Be Powerful Beyond Measure
and Intentionally Manifest What
You Want, is to make the REST of
your LIFE, the BEST of your LIFE.

~#43~

To Be Powerful Beyond Measure
and Intentionally Manifest What
You Want, is to strive to be better
than the person you were yesterday.

~#44~

To Be Powerful Beyond Measure
and Intentionally Manifest What
You Want, is to Anticipate Nothing
and Appreciate Everything.

~#45~

To Be Powerful Beyond Measure
and Intentionally Manifest What
You Want, is to Always and in All
Ways be YOUnique, YOUthful and
beYOUtiful.

~#46~

To Be Powerful Beyond Measure
and Intentionally Manifest What
You Want, is to Let what you Say
(Voice) become what you See
(Vision) to become what you Show
(Value).

~#47~

To Be Powerful Beyond Measure
and Intentionally Manifest What
You Want, is to know you were born
to be Great and do Greater so others
will Greatly appreciate your
Greatness

~#48~

To Be Powerful Beyond Measure
and Intentionally Manifest What
You Want, is to **PRAISE**
Yourself...**P**rotect your Plan.
Realize your Potential.
Acknowledge your Progress.
Illuminate your Presence. **S**tand in
your Purpose. **E**nvision your
Promises.

~#49~

To Be Powerful Beyond Measure
and Intentionally Manifest What
You Want, is to Awaken and
Acknowledge your Awesome
Authentic self is to "ACT AS IF"
instead of asking "What If?"...it is
never too late.

~#50~

To Be Powerful Beyond Measure
and Intentionally Manifest What
You Want, is to You Conceive of a
thing; you Believe in that thing; you
Perceive the reality of that thing;
you Achieve quality with that thing
and you Receive that thing in your
experience -- according to your
thoughts and beliefs.

RELEASE THE GREATNESS WITHIN

~#1~

To Be Powerful Beyond Measure
and Release The Greatness Within,
is to know there is no Success
without Sweat and Sacrifice.

~#2~

To Be Powerful Beyond Measure
and Release The Greatness Within,
is to Focus 100% in a deliberate,
conscious way to manifest what you
want into your life.

~#3~

To Be Powerful Beyond Measure
and Release The Greatness Within,
is to know that Attention is the
magnet that will Manifest what you
Intend and Expect.

~#4~

To Be Powerful Beyond Measure
and Release The Greatness Within,
is to know things are not only
possible...they are achievABLE,
availABLE, believABLE, doABLE,
managABLE and probABLE. You
are capABLE because God IS ABLE.

~#5~

To Be Powerful Beyond Measure
and Live Your Life's Purpose, is to
know BIG Expectations will
manifest big Revelations.

~#6~

To Be Powerful Beyond Measure
and Release The Greatness Within,
is to know Love is an irresistible
desire to be irresistibly desired.

~#7~

To Be Powerful Beyond Measure and Release The Greatness Within, is to Live your life on Purpose, with a Purpose and for a Purpose by an Established Foundation; Executed Focus; Elevated Faith; Expected Favor and Experienced Fulfillment.

~#8~

To Be Powerful Beyond Measure and Release The Greatness Within, is to walk in new fields of Divine Activity that are now open for you.

~#9~

To Be Powerful Beyond Measure
and Release The Greatness Within,
is to know your good now flows to
you in a steady unbroken, ever
increasing stream of Love,
Happiness, Success, Abundance
and Favor.

~#10~

To Be Powerful Beyond Measure
and Release The Greatness Within,
is to know you are better and better
with every thought you think, every
word you speak, everything you
do... EVERYDAY IN EVERYWAY!!!

~#11~

To Be Powerful Beyond Measure
and Release The Greatness Within,
is to possess an Attitude of
Gratitude. God has brand-new
blessings for you and you ought to
find yourself being grateful for the
Plans, Positions, Possibilities,
Promises, Promotions, Provisions
and Purposes to be manifested in
your life.

~#12~

To Be Powerful Beyond Measure
and Release The Greatness Within,
is to have the ability to believe in
yourself and 'BELIEVE IT IN' what
might ordinarily seem impossible.

~#13~

To Be Powerful Beyond Measure
and Release The Greatness Within,
is to be someone worth knowing
and not just someone who is well-
known.

~#14~

To Be Powerful Beyond Measure is to be Persistent and Consistent, Passionate and Compassionate to Intentionally Manifest What You Want.

~#15~

To Be Powerful Beyond Measure and Release The Greatness Within, is to know when life tries to take you down to a whisper, take it back up with a SHOUT.

~#16~

To Be Powerful Beyond Measure
and Release The Greatness Within,
is to flourish in a Nourishing and
Nurturing atmosphere.

~#17~

To Be Powerful Beyond Measure
and Release The Greatness Within,
is to Release and Relinquish the old
to Receive the new!

~#18~

To Be Powerful Beyond Measure
and Release The Greatness Within,
is to know the Bible does not say
"You will have what THEY say." It
says "You will have what YOU say."

~#19~

To Be Powerful Beyond Measure
and Release The Greatness Within,
is to focus what is holding you
together instead of what is tearing
you apart.

~#20~

To Be Powerful Beyond Measure
and Release The Greatness Within,
is to know your eyes are in front
because it is more important to look
ahead than to look back. Do not
dwell on things in the past.

~#21~

To Be Powerful Beyond Measure
and Release The Greatness Within,
is to choose to move on and put it
Behind you and not let negative
circumstances or situations Confine
you, Define you, Outshine you or
Refine you.

~#22~

To Be Powerful Beyond Measure is to unleash the Greatness within to Intentionally Manifest What You Want.

~#23~

To Be Powerful Beyond Measure and Release The Greatness Within, is to know in order to unlock the Power (Blessings), you have to embrace the Principles (Bible).

~#24~

To Be Powerful Beyond Measure
and Release The Greatness Within,
is to Consistently be Grateful and
Gracious...Always and in All Ways.

~#25~

To Be Powerful Beyond Measure
and Release The Greatness Within,
is to write new chapters of your life
and stop reading and re-reading the
old ones.

~#26~

To Be Powerful Beyond Measure
and Release The Greatness Within,
is to not put the key to your DOOR
(Destiny, Optimism, Originality,
Reality) and LOCK (Life,
Opportunities, Confidence,
Knowledge) in someone else's
pocket.

~#27~

To Be Powerful Beyond Measure
and Release The Greatness Within,
is to be EXTRAORDINARY. It is
that simple.

~#28~

To Be Powerful Beyond Measure
and Release The Greatness Within,
is to make the statement "God
Can!" instead of asking the question
'Can God?'

~#29~

To Be Powerful Beyond Measure
and Release The Greatness Within,
is to stop Thinking of what could go
wrong and start Thanking of what
could go right.

~#30~

To Be Powerful Beyond Measure
and Release The Greatness Within,
is to let go of who you think you are
supposed to be and Embrace,
Engage, Enjoy and Expand who you
are.

~#31~

To Be Powerful Beyond Measure
and Release The Greatness Within,
is to Fight for and Focus on what
you Love, so you will forget and not
cry for what you have lost.

~#32~

To Be Powerful Beyond Measure
and Release The Greatness Within,
is to leave the past in the
past...Period.

~#33~

To Be Powerful Beyond Measure
and Release The Greatness Within,
is to never allow a passive voice
from your past prevent you from
the Persistent Pursuit of Victory in
your Present and Presence.

~#34~

To Be Powerful Beyond Measure
and Release The Greatness Within,
is to know God's "You Are" must
become your "I Am."

~#35~

To Be Powerful Beyond Measure
and Release The Greatness Within,
is to have WMD's (Weapons of
Mass Destruction)...Wisdom,
Wholeness, Worth; Meaning,
Mercy, Motivation; Determination,
Dignity and Desire.

~#36~

To Be Powerful Beyond Measure
and Release The Greatness Within,
is to Possess Passion, Patience,
Perseverance, Persistence, Positive
Perspective, Perspiration, Plan,
Potential, Power and Purpose to
Pursue all of your Possibilities.

~#37~

To Be Powerful Beyond Measure
and Release The Greatness Within,
is to possess the Flight, the Might,
the Right, and the Sight to do great
things, but you have to develop the
Fight.

~#38~

To Be Powerful Beyond Measure
and Release The Greatness Within,
is to BeLIVEing in Your Leadershift
+ TransforMEtion + EmpowerMEnt
= a YOUnique you.

~#39~

To Be Powerful Beyond Measure
and Release The Greatness Within,
is to know Extraordinary people do
daily what ordinary people do
occasionally. Be better by nature
than most are by practice.

~#40~

To Be Powerful Beyond Measure
and Release The Greatness Within,
is to know the world needs what you
have. Your purpose will change
lives. You were born On Purpose,
With a Purpose and For a Purpose.
Live Your Purpose.

~#41~

To Be Powerful Beyond Measure
and Release The Greatness Within,
is to know today is a Great day for
you to Thank YOU for being an
Awesome, Amazing, Confident,
Courageous, Diligent, Dynamic,
Enthusiastic, Generous, Loveable,
Magnificent, Productive,
Responsible, Significant, Talented,
Unique and Wonderful person.

~#42~

To Be Powerful Beyond Measure
and Release The Greatness Within,
is to know it is time to unDO the
things that are unACHIEVABLE,
unACCEPTABLE, unBELIEVABLE
and unINTENTIONAL.
UNderstand your UNiqueness.

~#43~

To Be Powerful Beyond Measure
and Release The Greatness Within,
is to know you have power over
your life YOU control things. You
are the one who determines how
Significant and Magnificent you will
be. You are the one who determines
how much, how far and how high
you will go/grow.

~#44~

To Be Powerful Beyond Measure
and Release The Greatness Within,
is to know the Attribute of your
Attitude Affects your Aptitude to
Amplify your Altitude.

~#45~

To Be Powerful Beyond Measure
and Release The Greatness Within,
is to have your Responsibility is to
Imagine, Impact, Improve,
Implement, Influence, Inform,
Intend and Inspire your
Opportunities and Possibilities.

~#46~

To Be Powerful Beyond Measure
and Release The Greatness Within,
is to know your Commentary is to
Consistently and Persistently in All
Ways and Always be an Actionary,
Complimentary, Extraordinary,
Legendary, Necessary and a
Visionary of your life.

~#47~

To Be Powerful Beyond Measure
and Release The Greatness Within,
is to be Gracious and Grateful;
Consistent and Persistent;
Compassionate and
Passionate...Always and in All
Ways.

~#48~

To Be Powerful Beyond Measure
and Release The Greatness Within,
is to know what you are handed,
you can handle.

~#49~

To Be Powerful Beyond Measure
and Release The Greatness Within,
is to know you are what your
deepest desire is. As your desire is,
so is your INTENTION. As your
Intention is, so is your
INFLUENCE. As your Influence is,
so is your ILLUMINATION. As your
Illumination is, so is your IMPACT.

~#50~

To Be Powerful Beyond Measure
and Release The Greatness Within,
is to know your Ambitions, Beliefs,
Dreams, Expectations, Faith, Focus
and Goals are and should be so BIG,
you feel uncomfortable telling small
minded people.

AN OPTIMISTIC OUTLOOK

~#1~

To Be Powerful Beyond Measure
and Have An Optimistic Outlook, is
to let LIFE love you
Unconditionally, Lift you
Unconventionally and Leads you
Uncommonly.

~#2~

To Be Powerful Beyond Measure
and Have An Optimistic Outlook, is
to BEcome what you believe.

~#3~

To Be Powerful Beyond Measure
and Have An Optimistic Outlook, is
to see the Opportunities in every
obstacle.

~#4~

To Be Powerful Beyond Measure
and Have An Optimistic Outlook, is
to be Fearlessly FEAR (Faith,
Empowered, Ambitious, Relentless)
FULL.

~#5~

To Be Powerful Beyond Measure
and Have An Optimistic Outlook, is
to not be content with the content.

~#6~

To Be Powerful Beyond Measure
and Have An Optimistic Outlook, is
to move out of your comfort zone.
You can only grow if you are willing
to feel awkward and uncomfortable
when you try something new.

~#7~

To Be Powerful Beyond Measure
and Have An Optimistic Outlook, is
to not think outside the box, but
think like there is no box.

~#8~

To Be Powerful Beyond Measure
and Have An Optimistic Outlook, is
to Believe you will Receive what you
pray for.

~#9~

To Be Powerful Beyond Measure
and Have An Optimistic Outlook, is
to Validate your own Value (What
You Show), Vision (What You See)
and Voice (What You Say).

~#10~

To Be Powerful Beyond Measure
and Have An Optimistic Outlook, is
to make the TransACTION to
release your DistrACTION to have
an AttrACTION to embrace your
life's SatisfACTION.

~#11~

To Be Powerful Beyond Measure
and Have An Optimistic Outlook, is
to Expect an Extraordinary
Environment where people feel
Energetic and Extraordinarily
Exceptional.

~#12~

To Be Powerful Beyond Measure
and Have An Optimistic Outlook, is
to make the conscious readjustment
of who you think you are, to who
you really are.

~#13~

To Be Powerful Beyond Measure
and Have An Optimistic Outlook, is
to beYOUtiful.

~#14~

To Be Powerful Beyond Measure
and Have An Optimistic Outlook, is
to possess an Attitude of Gratitude.

~#15~

To Be Powerful Beyond Measure
and Have An Optimistic Outlook, is
to know that God has a Plan and
Purpose for your life.

~#16~

To Be Powerful Beyond Measure
and Have An Optimistic Outlook, is
to know that the best views come
from the hardest climb.

~#17~

To Be Powerful Beyond Measure
and Have An Optimistic Outlook, is
to Articulate, Communicate and
Pontificate Everything you Expect
and Intend to be Manifested in your
life.

~#18~

To Be Powerful Beyond Measure
and Have An Optimistic Outlook, is
to know what you Believe and
Conceive in your "Goal Mind"
(head) you will Achieve and Receive
in your "Gold Mine" (hand).

~#19~

To Be Powerful Beyond Measure
and Have An Optimistic Outlook, is
to know while you are Praying, God
is Preparing.

~#20~

To Be Powerful Beyond Measure
and Have An Optimistic Outlook, is
to know your Direction is more
important than your location.

~#21~

To Be Powerful Beyond Measure
and Have An Optimistic Outlook, is
to FOCUS on Uplifting things
instead of unwanted things.

~#22~

To Be Powerful Beyond Measure
and Have An Optimistic Outlook is
in your BELIEF - Be Everything Life
Intended, Expect Fulfillment.

~#23~

To Be Powerful Beyond Measure
and Have An Optimistic Outlook, is
to Keep Planting, Plowing,
Producing, Pouring and Pruning.
Life Is Giving You A Powerful,
Plentiful and Prosperous Harvest.

~#24~

To Be Powerful Beyond Measure
and Have An Optimistic Outlook, is
to make the conscious readjustment
to Appreciate, Create, Facilitate and
Regulate the life you Intend to have.

~#25~

To Be Powerful Beyond Measure
and Have An Optimistic Outlook, is
to Always and in All Ways be
Significant and Magnificent to
people who will be a Recipient.

~#26~

To Be Powerful Beyond Measure
and Have An Optimistic Outlook, is
to remember the same God that
made a way the last time, will make
a way this time and the next time.

~#27~

To Be Powerful Beyond Measure
and Have An Optimistic Outlook, is
to know just because they are in
your circle does not mean they are
in your corner.

~#28~

To Be Powerful Beyond Measure
and Have An Optimistic Outlook, is
to CHOOSE to Deliberately,
Intentionally and Proactively live
your life fully and exceptionally the
way you deserve.

~#29~

To Be Powerful Beyond Measure
and Have An Optimistic Outlook, is
to shOUT knowing God has already
worked OUT what you are worrying
abOUT.

~#30~

To Be Powerful Beyond Measure
and Have An Optimistic Outlook, is
to be better by nature than others
are by practice.

~#31~

To Be Powerful Beyond Measure and Have An Optimistic Outlook, is to minimized fear in how far you have come and maximize Faith in how far you will go!

~#32~

To Be Powerful Beyond Measure and Have An Optimistic Outlook, is to know your past is your Experience; your present is your Experiment and your future is your Expectation.

~#33~

To Be Powerful Beyond Measure
and Have An Optimistic Outlook, is
to Seize this moment to be in place
to secure the next moment.

~#34~

To Be Powerful Beyond Measure
and Have An Optimistic Outlook, is
to know Magnificent and Significant
people do not do extraordinary
things, but they do ordinary things
in an extraordinary way.

~#35~

To Be Powerful Beyond Measure
and Have An Optimistic Outlook, is
to Exercise You Faith that causes
you to Pray and Excuse your fear
that causes you to panic.

~#36~

To Be Powerful Beyond Measure
and Have An Optimistic Outlook, is
to grow (go) through to grow (go)
into.

~#37~

To Be Powerful Beyond Measure
and Have An Optimistic Outlook, is
to know you did not come this far to
only come this far.

~#38~

To Be Powerful Beyond Measure
and Have An Optimistic Outlook, is
to move from Survival to Stability,
from Stability to Success, from
Success to Significant.

~#39~

To Be Powerful Beyond Measure
and Have An Optimistic Outlook, is
to Pray about it more than you talk
about it.

~#40~

To Be Powerful Beyond Measure
and Have An Optimistic Outlook, is
to know it is not so much where you
are going, it is what you are willing
to let go of to get there!

~#41~

To Be Powerful Beyond Measure
and Have An Optimistic Outlook, is
to have Faith to 'BELIEVE IT IN',
Focus to 'CONCEIVE IT IN' and
Favor to 'RECEIVE IT IN'.

~#42~

To Be Powerful Beyond Measure
and Have An Optimistic Outlook, is
to walk with God in the dark than
go alone in the light.

~#43~

To Be Powerful Beyond Measure and Have An Optimistic Outlook, is to know Life WILL give you ALL that you Anticipate, Believe, Create, Expect, Intend, Need, Plan for and Want.

~#44~

To Be Powerful Beyond Measure and Have An Optimistic Outlook, is to know your clique should help you maintain your **CLICK**... **C**haracter, **L**ove, **I**ntegrity, **C**onfidence & **K**nowledge.

~#45~

To Be Powerful Beyond Measure and Have An Optimistic Outlook, is to know God DESIGNS what we go through but we DECIDE how we go through it.

~#46~

To Be Powerful Beyond Measure and Have An Optimistic Outlook, is to know your Ambitions, Beliefs, Dreams, Expectations, Faith, Focus and Goals are and should be so BIG, you feel uncomfortable telling small minded people.

~#47~

To Be Powerful Beyond Measure
and Have An Optimistic Outlook, is
to Intend in your life an Abundant
Abundance, Expected Expectancy,
Increased Increase and Overflowing
Overflow of Unprecedented Favor
in your Heart (Love), Head
(Learning) and Hand (Labor).

~#48~

To Be Powerful Beyond Measure
and Have An Optimistic Outlook, is
to Reach Upward, Open Inward so
you can Expand Outward to awaken
your Authentic, Original,
Custom/Tailor-Made, One-Of-A-
Kind Self. Expect to Expand and
Expand to Expect.

~#49~

To Be Powerful Beyond Measure
and Have An Optimistic Outlook, is
to know if you can see it, you can
BEcome it.

~#50~

Your Utmost Highest is to Express
and Possess A Focused and Positive
Mind, A Sense of Purpose, Clarity,
Creative Ability, Courage,
Charisma, Consistency,
Determination, Energy, Intentional,
Inner Peace, Inner Strength,
Passion for Life, Persistence,
Resilience, Self-Confidence, Self-
Esteem and Self-Worth.